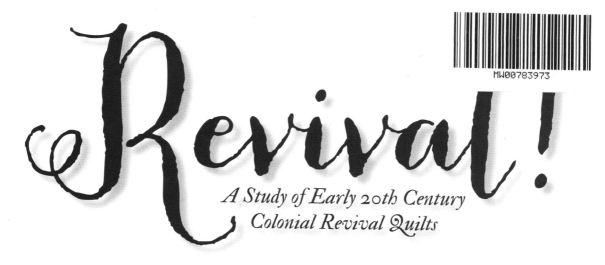

Revival!

A Study of Early 20th Century Colonial Revival Quilts

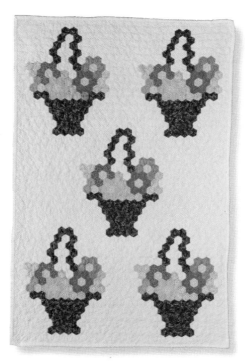

By the AMERICAN QUILT STUDY GROUP

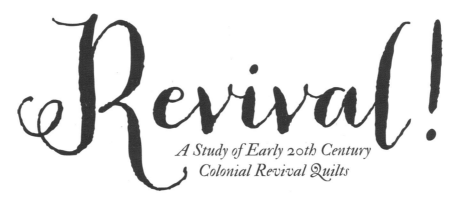

Revival!

A Study of Early 20th Century Colonial Revival Quilts

By the AMERICAN QUILT STUDY GROUP

EDITOR: Deb Rowden
DESIGNER: Bob Deck
PHOTOGRAPHY: Aaron T. Leimkuehler
ILLUSTRATION: Lon Eric Craven
TECHNICAL EDITOR: Jane Miller
PRODUCTION ASSISTANCE: Jo Ann Groves

PUBLISHED BY:
Kansas City Star Books
1729 Grand Blvd.
Kansas City, Missouri, USA 64108

First edition, first printing
ISBN: 978-1-61169-085-9

LIBRARY OF CONGRESS CONTROL NUMBER: 2013933476

Printed in the United States of America by Walsworth Publishing Co., Marceline, MO

To order copies, call StarInfo at (816) 234-4242 and say "Books."

DEDICATION

We dedicate this book to the anonymous early 20th century quiltmakers who left us so many wonderful quilts to research, collect and cherish. We are also grateful for the researchers who came before us and felt that quilts and their makers were important enough to document.

ACKNOWLEDGEMENTS

This book is a true labor of love by many people who love quilt history. Countless hours of work were contributed by members of the American Quilt Study Group: the volunteers who coordinated this project, the members who dreamed up and created the quilts, and the dedicated people who helped put this book together.

We could not exist without AQSG's Judy J. Brott Buss, Executive Director and Anne E. Schuff, Member Services Coordinator for their dedication and effort truly above and beyond.

Thanks to all of you!

CREDITS

All project instructions were written by Lisa Erlandson, current AQSG president.

CONTENTS

Introduction..4

Traveling Exhibit Schedule..4

The 2012 AQSG Quilt Study: Early 20th Century Colonial Revival Quilts........5

Guidelines for the 2012 Quilt Study..8

Colonial Revival Study Quilts...9

Patterns..44

About AQSG...96

INTRODUCTION

By Lisa Erlandson

Welcome to the Revival! The quilts featured in this book are the result of the 2012 Quilt Study project and were created by members of the American Quilt Study Group. The challenge presented in the 20th Century Colonial Revival Quilt Study: make a new quilt inspired by a quilt made during the early part of the 20th century.

Twenty-eight quilts were created, 15 of which are traveling to exhibit venues around the country. Please look for a location near you and see these quilts in person! The American Quilt Study Group is pleased to be able to bring these exhibits to you. AQSG invites you to explore quilt research and learn more about quilts, their past, present and future. You can read more about AQSG – who we are, how we came about, and how you can join us – on page 96.

In the pages that follow, you will see each quilt and read about the process each maker experienced from choosing the inspiration quilt to the completion of the study quilt. The guidelines for the Quilt Study are also included (page 8) to help you further understand the reasons behind the choices and the creations. Also in these pages, you will find patterns for 10 of these quilts so you can experience some of the journey along with the Quilt Study participants.

This is the 7th biennial Quilt Study offered by AQSG. The purpose of the Quilt Study is to offer members the chance to study a particular quilt from a given time period and/or style. This study is not just with books, paper and computers, but a hands-on study examining the quilt, the pattern, the fabrics, the way the quilts were constructed and quilted. If it is true that we learn best by doing, the AQSG members who have participated in the Quilt Studies have learned and shared in the best way possible!

Lisa Erlandson is an AQS Certified Appraiser of Quilted Textiles, lecturer, quilt show judge, teacher and quilt historian. She has served on the AQSG Board of Directors and is the 2012-2013 AQSG President.

TRAVELING EXHIBIT SCHEDULE

Monroe County History Center/Indiana Heritage Quilt Show, Bloomington, IN
February 2013-June 2013

International Quilt Study Center and Museum, Lincoln, NE
June/July 2013 -late 2013

Quilter's Hall of Fame, Marion, IN
April 2014-July 2014

New England Quilt Museum, Lowell, MA
July 2014-Fall 2014 (includes Lowell Quilt Festival)

Sheerar Museum of Stillwater History, Stillwater, OK
November 2014 – March 2015

Maine Quilts, hosted by the Pine Tree Quilters Guild, Augusta, ME
July 2015

For an updated list, visit WWW.AMERICANQUILTSTUDYGROUP.ORG

The 2012 AQSG Quilt Study:
Early 20th Century Colonial Revival Quilts

By Merikay Waldvogel

The Quilt Revival of the 1920s and 1930s resulted in untold numbers of people trying their hands at quilt making for the first time. They had time and money to spare, so why not make a quilt!

In doing so, they were reviving a long-held tradition with deep roots in American history. Marie Webster, in her 1915 quilt book *Quilts, Their Story and How To Make Them*, equated quilt making with national pride. The quilt revival, she wrote, "should be a source of much satisfaction to all patriotic Americans who believe that the true source of our nation's strength lies in keeping the family hearth flame bright." [1]

Nostalgic 20th century quilt advertisements linked the making of quilts to America's colonial past. Never mind that the quilts advertised might be strikingly modern or even a kit quilt, the making of quilts harkened back to a pre-industrial time. For quilts and quilt making, the "Colonial Revival" message implied old-fashioned, homespun, and noble.

This 2012 AQSG quilt study challenge – Colonial Revival Quilts of the Early 20th Century – required that each entrant choose a quilt from the 1920s and 1930s. The organizers sidestepped the issue of what is a Colonial Revival quilt and what is not, but some final entries have Revolutionary War battle names and stylistic motifs connected with Early American needlework such as baskets, flowers, and ribbons. In fact, Colonial Revival

THE PATCHWORK BOOK

NEEDLECRAFT MAGAZINE

might have been the undercurrent, but the quilt revival brought forth so much more than a re-introduction of old fashioned styles and the AQSG quilt study entries reflect that diversity.

In 1929, Stearns & Foster Co., maker of Mountain Mist batting, introduced a line of quilt patterns in both modern and traditional styles. Their national advertising in women's magazines in the 1930s reached one in three households, according to the company. Column-wide ads headed by testimonials from satisfied quilters such as, "It's an Antique pattern, but I made it" or "In the good ole days everyone made a Dozen quilts" were designed to tap into the Colonial Revival fervor.

Entrepreneurs of all sizes took notice of rising interest in making quilts. Twentieth century quilt designers such as Marie Webster (Marion, Indiana) and Anne Orr (Nashville, Tennessee) wrote for women's magazines distributed throughout the nation. Marie Webster's designs appeared in *Ladies Home Journal* and *Needlecraft* magazine. Anne Orr, as needlework editor of *Good Housekeeping* magazine, devoted at least one column per year to her quilt designs. Both women had studio workshops in their homes where a staff of seamstresses and designers produced quilt patterns and quilt kits.

Marie Webster revived the center medallion appliqué style of the middle 19th century but her floral

[1] Marie Webster, *Quilts, Their Story and How to Make Them* (1915), xvi.

renditions were more realistic than the earlier folk-style appliqué. For example, her poppies and tulips bent and swayed as if windblown. She chose solid pastel colors for the flowers to be applied on a white foundation fabric.

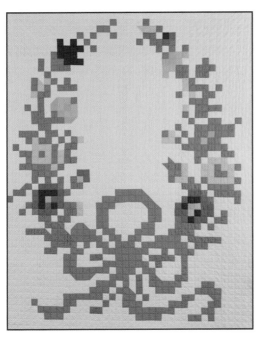

Anne Orr also created a line of appliqué medallion quilts, but her signature designs were constructed of hundreds of small cotton squares in a gridded format. Derived from needlepoint and tatting designs, the beribboned wreaths or vases of flowers in her quilt designs convey a "Colonial Revival" theme.

Both women's quilt designs were sophisticated, but complicated. Besides packaged kits, they also sold partially completed quilt projects as well as completed quilts. Kits, basted quilts and finished quilts cost more, of course, but they saved time. Much larger thread companies also offered quilt kits in the early 1930s. By making the whole process simpler and more enjoyable, they hoped to reach the middle-class woman new to quilting.

Another strong motivation to make a quilt in the 1930s was to reconstruct a family heirloom quilt.

Some families lost their 19th century quilts through wars, migration, and harsh conditions. Others still had the quilt, but it was worn beyond repair. Some quilters had a scrap bag to delve into, but others shopped for reproduction fabrics. Any quilt made in a large four-block floral appliqué made in the popular red, green, pink, and yellow colors of the mid-1800s is probably a family's reproduction quilt.

Household magazine in April 1934 advertised a pattern for a variation of the very popular scrap quilt Trip Around the World. Along with the pattern, the company offered to send a one-pound package of new materials in pattern prints for two one-year subscriptions to the magazine costing just $1.00. *Grit* magazine in 1935 described its Trip Around the World project as good "pick up" work when callers come and reminded its readers that ". . . sewing by hand is always the better way since it is a reproduction of an old quilt."

Throughout the 1930s quilt revival, the call for quilt patterns was insatiable. Newspapers became a ready

source of low-cost patterns. Publishers of franchised quilt columns, such as Laura Wheeler/Alice Brooks based in New York City, supplied quilt patterns to local newspapers throughout the United States. The artists and editors for this column seemed well-attuned to the quilting traditions of long-time quilters. They offered modern patterns for scrap quilts and encouraged "friendship" quilting together. A pattern sheet with instructions cost ten cents.

Long-time quilters no doubt appreciated the new patterns, but paying any amount for a mail-order pattern was just unthinkable. Instead, they drafted their own blocks using the illustrations provided by newspapers and cut their own templates from box tops or sandpaper. Others combined patterns, border treatments, and quilting designs in one quilt.

Farm magazines such as *Capper's Weekly* based in Topeka, Kansas, had a much farther reach than a local paper. Louise Fowler Root, writing for *Capper's*, offered updated traditional patterns. "Spring Time in the Rockies" is clearly an adaptation of the mid-19th century quilt pattern Rocky Mountain Road or Crown of Thorns. Stearns & Foster Co. renamed it "New York Beauty" in 1930, but Louise Fowler Root said it

reminded her of the "glorious sunrises one sees in the mountains while the green and white stripes were mountain pathways with the spring's first green grass peeping through the snow."

All the AQSG Study Quilt participants met the requirements: choosing an inspiration quilt from the appropriate time period, reducing the new quilt to 200 inches for all four sides, and obtaining the owner's permission. Each entrant was asked to comment on the project. One woman wrote, "As I made my quilt, I thought of Olive. She must have loved to appliqué as I do. She must have certainly made thoughtful fabric choices and played with the placement of colors, just as I have."

Another woman wrote, "I had to admire the tenacity of a person who hand-quilted a one-inch grid after hand piecing 16 blocks of such a complicated pattern. I wonder if the original's maker had a sewing machine available. Could it be that the quiltmaker's choice of method had to do with keeping in the spirit of the romance of the Colonial Revival, with needle in hand rather than foot on a pedal?"

21st century quilters have dazzling technological inventions to make the quilting process easier. Quilting classes, patterns, and instruction books are available online. If you want to become a quilter, you can. When you do, you will be joining a long, proud line of quiltmakers. Take time to make a quilt the "old-fashioned" way. Learning from their efforts will enrich your own experience.

Merikay Waldvogel is a nationally known quilt authority and is best known for her published works on 1930s quiltmaking, including Soft Covers for Hard Times: Quiltmaking and the Great Depression *and* Patchwork Souvenirs of the 1933 Chicago World's Fair. *She served as a board member of the American Quilt Study Group and judged this Colonial Revival Quilt Challenge.*

GUIDELINES FOR THE 2012 QUILT STUDY

AQSG invited members to join in and create a reproduction quilt for the seventh biennial AQSG Quilt Study for the October 2012 Seminar in Lincoln, Nebraska. The focus of the 2012 Study: Quilts from the Colonial Revival of the Early 20th Century as a way of learning about our quilt heritage and to help promote AQSG.

The guidelines:

- For purposes of this Quilt Study, the Early 20th Century Quilt Revival is defined as quilts made during the 1920s and 1930s. The inspiration quilt must be clearly identifiable as a quilt from this time period.

- Participants may reproduce a portion of the original, or a scaled down version of any quilt of the period. Participants may make an exact replica of the original quilt, but it is not required. Participants may also make a quilt that is "inspired" by the original.

- Only AQSG Members may participate on any individual or group project. Each individual and/or group will be limited to submitting one quilt.

- An overall maximum measurement of 200 inches total for all four sides will be strictly enforced.

- To be considered a Quilt Study Participant, each individual or group must submit a completed and signed Participant Release, completed and signed Permission to Use Quilt Image or Photograph, a digital image in .jpg format of the inspiration quilt to the Quilt Study Committee from September 1, 2011, through September 1, 2012.

- For a quilt to be considered for a traveling exhibit, the completed and signed Participant Release, completed and signed Permission to Use Quilt Image or Photograph, a digital image in .jpg format of the inspiration quilt and the Written Statement must be submitted to the Quilt Study Committee no later than September 1, 2012. Additional quilts will be accepted for the exhibit as late as the installation date of the exhibit at Seminar, but only if exhibit space is available.

- The Participant Release and Permission to Use Quilt Image or Photograph forms should be obtained from the Quilt Study Committee.

- The photograph of the inspiration quilt must be in .jpg file format either as an email attachment or on a disk sent through the regular mail.

- The written statement must be submitted which states why the inspiration quilt was chosen, what approach was taken in making the new quilt and what was learned through participation in this Quilt Study. The written statement must be provided as a Word compatible document either as an email attachment or on a disk sent through the regular mail.

- A valuation of your finished quilt will be required prior to submission.

- Incomplete projects will not be accepted. All submitted quilts must be finished (i.e., quilted and bound). All submitted quilts must also have a 4" sleeve attached, and a label with your name and address sewn to a corner on the back of the quilt. An additional label with your entry number (when assigned) will also be required.

- Any quilt that does not fit within the guidelines of this study may not be considered for inclusion in the traveling exhibit.

Revival!
STUDY QUILTS

MARIA'S TREE OF LIFE

36" x 44"

Dale Drake
Martinsville, Indiana

Around ten years ago I was the lucky recipient of a complete Progress #1369 Tree of Life quilt kit in Depression-era pastel fabrics. I was entranced by the pattern, a classic example of Colonial Revivalism defined as "colonial" patterns reinterpreted in the popular colors of the time.

Progress was one of many quilt kit manufacturers active from the 1930s through the 1970s. These kits provided quiltmakers with inexpensive pre-designed quilts. In the article "Kit Quilts in Perspective" by Anne Copeland and Beverly Dunivent, published in *Uncoverings* 1995, the authors point out that these kits were a teaching tool in a time before quilt classes - although they were often far from simple. This pattern is one of the most complicated I have found, but it had a lasting appeal, being remarketed from 1966 to 1985 as Pattern #1492 with cotton/polyester calicoes in blues, olive green and gold. My kit includes a muslin background marked with appliqué placement lines and quilting pattern dots, plus hundreds of preprinted appliqué pieces.

For this project I needed to make a small version of the quilt. The purchase of a set of scanned images on a CD from an Ebay vendor (who was as enamored by the quilt as me) gave me my pattern. I printed the center medallion images at half size. I then mined my stash of vintage pastels, supplemented with Moda Bella Solids when necessary, and began the simple but lengthy process of tracing the pieces onto the colored fabrics, appliquéing them down, adding the embroidery accents and quilting the piece. The scalloped edge treatment completes the quilt, just as in the original.

For my inspiration quilt image, I searched the Quilt Index, finding many Tree of Life kit quilts made up in 1970s calicoes, and one beautifully photographed quilt in the pastel colors of my kit. Made by Maria Dolinsky Poholsky (1876-1954) in Pennsylvania in the 1940s, it was passed down through two generations and registered in the North Carolina Quilt Project in 1985 by Maria's granddaughter-in-law.

As I sewed my many appliqués down, fudging here and adjusting there to make things meet up, my admiration for Maria's perseverance grew. She had no extra fabric to re-cut a slightly larger piece; she had no flexibility of placement to cover up a mismatched flower petal. This project has given me new respect for the kit quiltmakers of the mid-20th century.

Photograph by Gregory R. Winter

A Thread of Memories

24" x 38"

Charletta Jokinen
Bloomington, Minnesota

I chose my inspiration quilt from the book *Minnesota Quilts, Creating Connections with Our Past*, published by Voyageur Press in 2005. This particular quilt was beautifully created by Zelda F. Graplar Detert in 1935. I knew the intricate pattern and flowing edges of this piece were going to be a challenge, but I was so drawn to her story and the picture of this masterpiece that I wanted to give it a try.

> "Quilt making experienced resurgence during the Depression. Patterns that made use of small pieces such as Grandmother's Flower Garden and Wedding Ring, were popular because bits of fabric from unworn old clothing were easy to come by; nothing was wasted. Many patterns were published around this time in newspapers and farm journals. Zelda created this design from the picture of a similar quilt she saw in *Farmer* magazine."
>
> — *Minnesota Quilts, Creating Connections with Our Past*

My design is both hand and machine quilted. I did replicate the basket of tulips but chose to apply a different pattern in the connecting squares. This was a labor of love in unfamiliar territory and I told my sister that 'I felt that I was in a foreign country and didn't speak the language.' She told me to go for it, and so I did.

I was excited to learn that the owner of this quilt was one of Zelda's daughters, Karen Mack of Viroqua, WI. Karen was so gracious and charming when I spoke with her that, by the time our conversation ended, I felt I knew her and her mother. As she spoke, I found that Zelda and I had a lot in common. Not only did Zelda raise her children, she enjoyed a large garden and loved to bake and cook for her family and friends.

Karen sent me a picture of her mother and to my delight told me some stories. My favorite is repeated in the *Minnesota Quilts* book, about Zelda:

> " ... participating in the tradition of bouncing a cat in the middle of the completed quilt; whichever girl the cat jumped nearest as it escaped the silliness would be the next to be married!"

I have great admiration for all the ladies that appliqué and do hand work. My sister makes it all look so easy and I found that it is not. This being my first attempt at hand-appliqué, I can only hope to get better with every stitch and continue the tradition of sharing my experience with my children and grandchildren. Who knows, maybe there is a Zelda in my family …

THE WILKINSON SISTERS REVISITED

41" x 40"

Marilyn Goldman
Selma, Indiana

I chose the Ligonier Public Library quilt for my inspiration because it was the first quilt made by the "Wilkinson Sisters" that I remember seeing. It was brought into an Indiana Quilt Registry Project discovery day to be photographed and documented. That was in 1987 - 25 years ago. Since then I have seen and worked on many more "Wilkinsons", but that first one stuck in my mind because it was so elegant.

For my study quilt, I used Prussian blue cotton sateen for the "A" side, which was a favorite fabric of the Wilkinson Sisters. I used a blush color for the "B" side, which was also authentic to the first quarter of the 20th century. The Wilkinson Sisters often used wool batting; however, I used cotton batting so it wouldn't shift if it had to hang a while. The thread is a blue Coats and Clark to match the "A" side, which is also what the Wilkinson Sisters used.

What I learned in this study of trying to replicate a "Wilkinson Sisters" quilt is that they and their quilters were master crafters. Scallops are hard to do! The binding on their scallops was smooth on the inside edge and pleated on the outside, which is a technique I have yet to master. Hand-drawn feathered frames are tricky. Crisp cross-hatching is mind-boggling!

Collection of Karen Dever

How Does Our Garden Grow?

45" x 41"

Karen Dever and Didi Salvatierra
Moorestown, New Jersey, and Bel Air, Maryland

Upon the announcement two years ago of the theme "Colonial Revival" for the 2012 AQSG Quilt Study, we knew that creating a botanical themed quilt would be a great project to work on together. We searched many quilts in our personal collections and the collections of museums and historical societies. We finally decided to use as our inspiration a quilt from Karen's personal collection – a circa 1940 Tulip Crib Quilt. The inspiration quilt represents characteristics of quilts from the Colonial Revival time period.

Karen acquired the original Tulip Crib Quilt from Cindy Rennels about eight years ago. Karen was able to locate a photograph of a similar quilt in the book, *A Garden of Quilts*, by Mary Elizabeth Johnson (1984, pp 34, 68). Information contained in the book indicates that the maker used a kit and added additional borders but there is no mention of a design source. Karen has continued researching the source of the kit through other quilt history researchers including Rosie Werner and Merikay Waldvogel.

However, no definitive source for the design of the original quilt has been located at this time.

Creating the quilt again to fit the size restrictions of the quilt study offered an opportunity to alter the design. Therefore, we decided to use the quilt as inspiration rather than replicating the original. Karen completed the top and Didi finished it with her beautiful quilting. The use of contemporary batiks brings the quilt design back to life and up to date in the 21st Century!

17

TO CLEARY WITH LOVE, FROM RUTH

43" x 48"

Jonda DeLozier
Bloomington, Minnesota

"To Cleary with Love, From Ruth" was inspired by a quilt lovingly given by a bride to her groom on their wedding day, September 19, 1931. Ruth and Cleary, who have since passed away, were my mother-in-law and father-in-law. This quilt still hangs on the wall as a much cherished family heirloom.

I chose to replicate the original appliqué and some of the quilting. To begin, I took a photo of the quilt and had an enlargement made to use as my master design. Having taken many appliqué technique classes over the years, I found the method that works best for me was taught by Karen Kay Buckley.

The key to Karen's method is Templar, a heat resistant plastic, and Magic Sizing. After the appliqué pieces are cut, the seams are turned by painting on the sizing (with a small brush), then pushed up over the edge of the template and pressed until dry. The Templar is removed and the shape is ready to be appliquéd.

I didn't have the privilege of knowing the maker of the quilt that inspired my project. The gift from my mother-in-law, Ruth, to her groom, Cleary, was actually made by her mother, Ida Dahl. From the stories I've heard, she was, as I am, a lifelong needlework artist. Over the years I have tried many needlework techniques, but quilting and embroidery are my favorite.

Upon examination of Ida's quilt, I think it might be her own design. The fact that it isn't symmetrical makes me think it is her creation or that she took inspiration from another quilter's work and made it her own. When I make quilts I put an unexpected "surprise" in each one (like using the back of a fabric), so I was excited to see that Ida had done the same. (See if you can find my surprise.) Besides being drawn to this quilt for its simplistic beauty, I feel connected to Ida for what I see as her sense of fun.

I thoroughly enjoyed the creation of my quilt, from design to construction. The biggest difference between what I anticipated and reality was the time involved. As I have experienced before, it always takes longer than expected, but I will definitely be doing more hand appliqué quilt projects.

Many thanks to Ida for her inspirational quilt, to Karen for her appliqué technique, and to my mom, Flora, for teaching me to sew. Love you, Mom.

GREAT GRANDMA LAURA'S SCRAP BASKETS

44 ½" x 45"

Terry Tickhill Terrell
Masonville, Colorado

My 2012 Study quilt, Great Grandma Laura's Scrap Baskets, was inspired by three quilts. The first was a 1930s era quilt top that I saw on an online auction site. The description read, "The quiltmaker was not afraid of color." The quiltmaker had pieced together colors with wild abandon, creating one of the most joyful quilts I had ever seen. Unfortunately I was not the successful bidder, but I made sketches of the quilt top with the plan to reproduce it one day. I searched unsuccessfully for the pattern—one with a pieced handle and seven triangles across the top row—for years. I eventually found a pillow (see inspiration photo) made from a fragment of a 1930s quilt made from the pattern for which I was searching. It provided an actual block from which I could draft a slightly smaller version.

My third source of inspiration was a quilt made for me in the 1950s by my great grandmother Laura Price Gibson when she was in her 80s and had been quilting for decades. I used that quilt not as a pattern but as an inspiration to combine colors with far greater freedom than usual. As I pieced my study quilt, I remembered watching Great Grandma Laura stitch my quilt.

I researched quilting motifs common during the Colonial Revival era - wreaths, pansies, and a nice sensible grid to tie them all together. The pansies were resized and copied from a 1930s appliqué pattern. I left some of my blue chalk markings on the piece just as a Colonial Revival era quilter would have done, knowing they would disappear in the first wash.

In the 1920s and '30s, patterns similar to mine were published. On October 24, 1928, The Kansas City Star published a pattern called Cherry Basket by Ruby Short McKim. It had a curved but not pieced handle and five triangles across the top row. Per Barbara Brackman's *Blockbase*: Pattern #669 Basket, published by *Grandmother Clark, Book 20* in 1931, has a pieced handle and five triangles across the top row. Another *Blockbase* Pattern #671 Flower Baskets, published by *Grandmother Dexter, Book 36a* in 1935, has a pieced handle and seven triangles across the top row. My pattern must have been published since I have found two unrelated examples of it, but I have yet to find it. I continue to search for the original pattern.

Colonial Belle Revisited

36" x 56"

Sharon Pinka
Bellville, Ohio
Quilting by Jessica Carnes

I selected my inspiration quilt because I wanted to try my hand at appliqué and was searching for a design reminiscent of the romantic feel of the Colonial Revival era. I remembered the picture of a quilt that my friend, Pat Lyons, sent me when she was trying to identify its source. We tracked down an illustration of the original pattern in a 1934 ad in *Household Magazine*. The magazine offered six free blocks with the purchase of two one-year subscriptions.

Rosie Werner then located some pictures of actual vintage blocks which helped me trace the designs of the six Colonial Belles. The patterns were also offered by *Grandmother Clark's* quilting designs and were titled "Poster Girls." The set of six white appliqué 18" square quilt blocks sold for 75 cents.

I did not copy the original entirely because I wanted to incorporate my own vintage fabrics and trims into the Belles' dresses and hats. Plus, I was not able to find the actual printed paper pattern, so I had to trace the ladies from completed blocks in existing quilts. Reproducing their faces proved more difficult than I anticipated, since I was actually reducing each figure to one-half size. Some of the eyes and noses contain only one or two stitches!

The similarities that I noticed between my quilt and the original included an obvious need for detail – my inspiration quilt contained 12 blocks and each was meticulously crafted down to the last eyelash, flower petal, and bow. The blocks deserved the attention that I tried to provide.

The main difference between the two quilts was that I had to adjust the original figures to one-half scale, necessitating the correct proportions of miniature prints and small trims.

I felt most connected with the maker while working on the embroidery in front of the TV, imagining my unknown compatriot taking her own stitches while listening to the radio during the 1930s.

My experience differed from my anticipated one in that I did not make my blocks as big as I should have, and had to adjust my sashing and border measurements accordingly. It also took much longer than I estimated to embroider the blocks – hats off to my inspiration quiltmaker who embroidered 12 colorful 18" blocks!

Tulip Stars - Batik Makeover Edition

30" x 30"

Sandra Starley
Moab, Utah

As a quilt appraiser, historian and lecturer, I am constantly on the lookout for fabulous quilts to add to my trunk show inventory. What better excuse for a purchase than the AQSG Quilt Revival Study. After participating in 2010, I was eager to try it again and quickly found an unusual vintage tulip quilt with a subtle star design (my favorite motif). But I kept looking – like Goldilocks, I didn't want to start sewing only to find the "just right" quilt the next week. I wanted a unique and interesting design from that era with strong visual appeal; not a well-known appliqué or popular pattern.

The main pattern of the inspiration quilt is "Mountain Star" from Home Needlecraft Creations, a kit quilt but not a common design. I've since found several examples, all with the same colors, block arrangement and quilting patterns but none with the giant tulip border so it is unique after all. With the clearly different workmanship, it appears that a later quilter added the border to frame the piece. It was a rather clunky fix, which I didn't want to duplicate yet I didn't quite want to lose the funky flavor. A piano key border with some of the fabrics that didn't make it into the flowers is, I hope, a more visually pleasing 'frame' that doesn't overwhelm the central design but adds interest to the appliqué pattern.

At over 20", the original blocks were bigger than many of my finished quilts, so I reduced them to 10" blocks. Of course, that made the pieces much smaller so I simplified the pattern from 87 to a mere 51 hand appliqué pieces per block. Then I moved on to fabric

selection. I'm a 19th century girl and have lots of reproduction fabrics from that century but not many from the 1930s. So while I often closely reproduce my inspiration quilts, this time it was fun to jazz things up with contemporary fabrics. I kept the basic color palette of the original but updated it with saturated batiks and a lightly printed background for a fresh modern feel.

With the countless hours spent on design decisions, I understand why this is called a quilt *study* and I'm beginning to see the appeal of kit quilts.

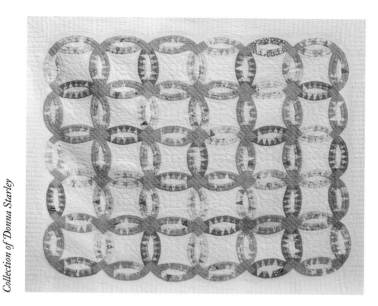

PICKLED GEESE

40" x 40"

Donna Starley
Logan, Utah

I was so excited for the Colonial Revival Quilt Study! Immediately, I began to search for "my" inspirational quilt. I knew instantly when I stumbled upon it! It was love at first sight! With inspirational quilt selected and secured, next I began one of my most arduous and intimidating quilting challenges. I spent a few months (to be honest, a year) "fretting" over drafting, designing, and constructing the elements of the Pickle Dish pattern. In my mind, I knew exactly what I wanted, but I just wasn't sure how to create it. I studied every Pickle Dish and Double Wedding Ring quilt and pattern I could find. I did endless searches on the web. I purchased and read books about Pickle Dishes and Wedding Rings (many of which were out of print). I designed and redrafted a myriad Pickle Dish patterns. I started sewing two different variations of these patterns. Some might say I was "obsessed," but I'm a counselor in my real life. I know the difference between "fretting" and "obsessing."

I was amazed at the number of design decisions critical in creating a Pickle Dish. During this grueling process, I debated the angles of the arcs, the width of the arcs, the length of the arcs, the number of pickles in the arcs, the angles of the pickles in the arcs, the intersections of the arcs, and even the visual impact of squares versus kite shaped pieces in the intersections. I even pondered if the arcs and intersections should form circles that were circular, or circles with flat tops, sides, and bottoms. Now remember . . . this is still just "fretting", NOT "obsessing."

Finally, after a year of researching, redesigning, multiple stops and starts, and perhaps even a little

procrastinating, I returned to "my" inspirational quilt and drafted it – exactly! I discovered in this challenging, yet enlightening process that I couldn't find or create an arc, a circle, or even a pickle that I liked more than the quilt I fell in love with a year earlier.

So, did I put a little of me in this challenge quilt? Yes! You may not be able to see all the time spent designing, planning, and rethinking this challenge. But you will see the geese flying in a few circles, and the metallic fabrics that give new life and sparkle to the original 1930s color palette.

MY ROSE GARDEN FOR MARY AND MARIE

24" x 42"

Marti Phelps
Prince Frederick, Maryland

I have always wanted to create a Marie Webster quilt. I have admired her as "Queen" of the Colonial Revival for years. Her medallion set designs have been my favorite, so I chose as my inspiration the "Morning Glory Wreath" quilt that she made for her granddaughter, Rosalind Webster Perry. My inspiration quilt appears on page 54 of Rosalind's second book, *Marie Webster's Garden of Quilts*.

I want my quilt to tell a story, and so I have decided to tell the story of another "flower lover," Mary Custis Lee, wife of Robert E. Lee. She had a beautiful rose garden at her home in Virginia, Arlington House. Sadly the home was taken away from her during the Civil War. She was a quilter and would have loved Marie Webster's quilts also, especially Marie's roses. Therefore, the name of my quilt is "My Rose Garden for Mary and Marie."

My inspiration quilt featured morning glories. My thoughts of Mary and Marie led me to roses instead. I researched the different rose patterns that Marie included in her quilts over the years. My roses are machine appliquéd using the freezer-paper turned-under edge technique. My new challenge was the fabric that I used. I love Radiance from Robert

Kaufman fabrics, a silk/cotton blend. I had never used it before for appliqué shapes or narrow stems. It cooperated nicely.

I like to machine quilt before I machine appliqué when possible so I do not have a lot of starts and stops in the quilting. The hand quilters in Marie's day did their appliqué first and then were able to quilt long lines of hand quilting. Hand quilting is still my favorite look, however for those of us in the 21st century it seems there are "so many quilts, but so little time." How did our predecessors ever find the time?

My little quilt has been a labor of love as I think of Mary and Marie's love for roses. I wish they could have discussed their fondness for flowers together. Their lives did overlap for a few years - Mary Lee passed away in 1873 when Marie Webster was 14 years old.

Thank you AQSG for the opportunity to participate in the quilt study.

Trip Around The World

20 ½" x 23 ¼"

Phyllis Stewart
Castle Rock, Colorado

I am very fortunate to come from a long line of quilters. I feel most fortunate to also be semi-related to a special Nebraska quilter named Mary Ghormley. She and Roger were good friends with my parents, and in 1967 my brother married their daughter. I guess that makes us "shirttail" relatives. As I grew up, we would spend time at the Ghormley home. I was amazed and impressed with all the quilts, especially her doll beds and doll quilts.

When I heard the 2012 quilt study theme would be about Colonial Revival quilts, I immediately went to a book about Mary Ghormley's quilts titled *Childhood Treasures*, by Merikay Waldvogel (2008). I found a wonderful "Trip Around the World" quilt. When I emailed Mary to ask permission, she reminded me that all those quilts were no longer hers; they belonged to the IQSC and she suggested that I write them. Janet Price from IQSC was able to give permission. In the meantime I began collecting reproductions from the 1930s that resembled the fabrics of the quilt in the book.

It is such a connection to the past to make a quilt and wonder why the quilter chose those particular fabrics. Were they leftovers from a large quilt that she made? Were they special fabrics left from making something for her daughter? Was the quilt used to cover a little doll or a teddy bear? Unfortunately we'll never know the true story behind this original, but I was certainly happy to think about it while I pieced my little doll quilt.

The original quilt had no batting or quilting – maybe because the maker just wanted it to drape and wrap nicely around a little girl's doll. When I made my reproduction, I put in a few rows of quilting just to hold the front and back together. Otherwise I tried to make mine look just as much like hers as possible, although she hand pieced and I used my rotary cutter to cut the squares and then my Bernina to sew them together. I copied her style of binding by bringing the back to the front and machine stitched it in place as she did.

What a joy this little journey has been. I can only hope that one day someone in a future generation finds one of my little original doll quilts and wants to reproduce it too. If so, they will find my name and date on the back!

THE FRENCH WREATH

45" x 55"

Gale Slagle
Irvine, California

After researching kit quilts for a quilt study presentation, I became intrigued with the Anne Orr graphic style quilts. Although they were modeled after cross-stitch patterns, they reminded me of pixilated Photoshop projects.

Anne Orr presented her first cross-stitch style quilt pattern in 1933 and continued to publish this style of quilt patterns into the 1940s. My friend Sandy Sutton owned an Anne Orr "French Wreath" quilt that I used as my study quilt. A picture of this quilt is also on the cover of *Uncoverings* 1990.

I used Photoshop to map out and design my pattern. I decided to use only the central wreath of the quilt in my study quilt. In addition, I changed a few of the flower shapes and decreased the size of the borders. This quilt is made from 2000 squares all cut to the same size. My squares were cut at 1 ½" inches to finish at 1".

Lockport Batting and Anne Orr had published some of Anne Orr's patterns in 1944 and Dover reprinted these patterns in 1990. In the pattern books it is recommended to work with a 10 x 10 grid. However, I choose to strip piece 5 – 1 ½" rows/strips together as much as possible to save time. Therefore, I ended up working with a 5 x 10 grid.

When I had pieced 10 rows of 5 squares together, I joined them to another 5 x 10 square unit making a 10 x 10 block of 1" squares. To match the seams I used a three pin method that I had learned from watching an episode of "Simply Quilts" a long time ago. One pin is used to hold the seams together. Then the other two pins are placed so one is on each side of the seam. Then the center pin is removed before sewing. After stitching the 20 – 10 x 10 blocks together I added a 5" border. The quilt was machine quilted in a simple grid pattern.

One thing I learned from this project is that stitching together 2000 squares takes a lot longer than one would think.

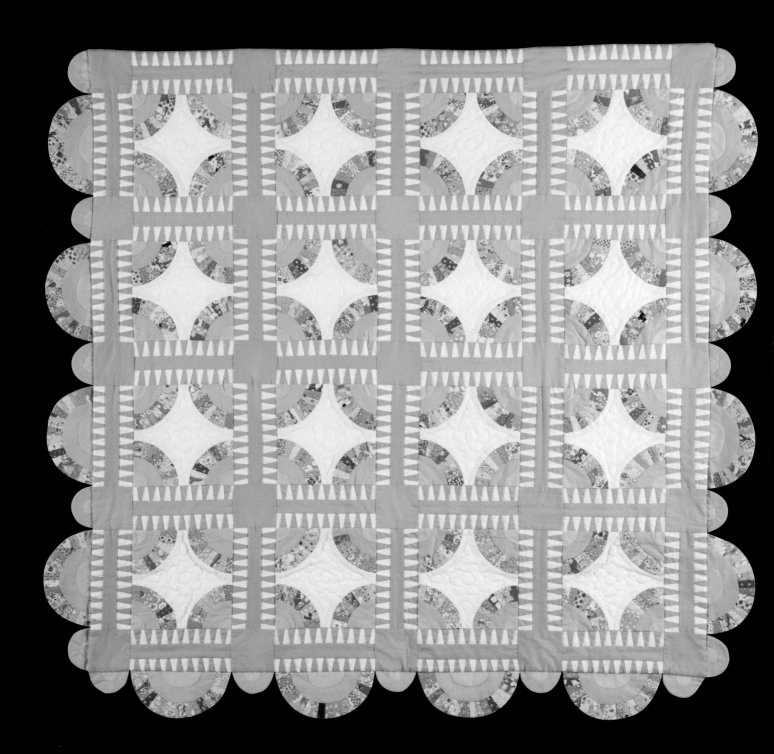

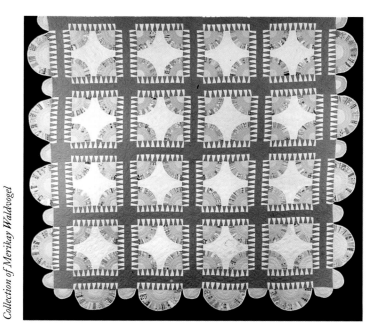

ROCKY MOUNTAIN SPRINGTIME

46" x 49"

Sherry Burkhalter
Newville, Alabama

This variation of a New York Beauty pattern was published in a 1931 article in *Capper's Weekly* titled "Springtime in the Rockies." It is a scrap quilt that also utilizes solid color fabric, which gives it both contrast and continuity. Sarah Moore of Meigs County, Tennessee, possibly made the quilt, circa 1934, as noted in *Soft Covers for Hard Times* by Merikay Waldvogel (1990).

The curved piecing is a change from the ordinary straight line piecing most often seen. Carrying the curves in the blocks out into the border makes it unusual and these extending curves on three sides of the quilt show it was to be used as a bed quilt. Foundation piecing made short work of the pieced curves and strips. It made me wonder if Sarah used a paper foundation as well - possibly pages of a catalogue or magazine.

Collecting the fabrics for this quilt was fun. It was a challenge to see how many fabrics could be found. The quilt contains more than 200 different reproduction fabrics that are alive with action and animation. There were lots of flowers and geometric shapes, children playing, the toys they played with, the animals they loved, and more. Looking at all of the wonderful fabrics that make up a 1930s scrap quilt is a great experience, and it was also very reflective. It is amazing how happy the fabrics seem when you think of the difficulty that the families faced at that time. The fabrics had to be a welcome retreat when they worked on the quilts and tried not to dwell on their circumstances. It was a joy for me as well.

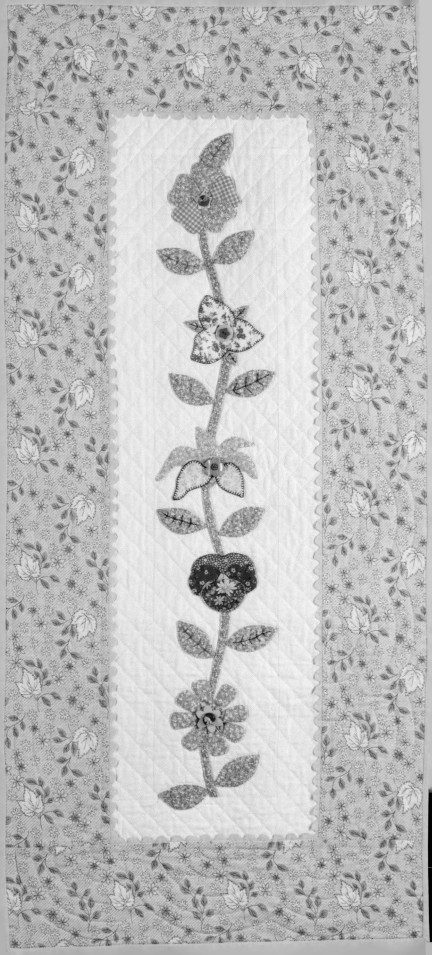

THE MAGIC VINE

22 ½" x 50"

Repiecers - A Southern California Quilt Study Group
*Marian Cassianni, Kay Ross, Sandy Sutton and
Leah Zieber*

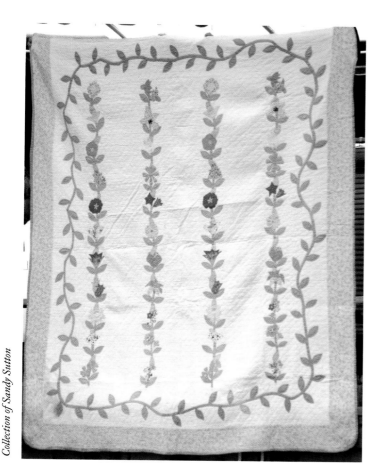

Collection of Sandy Sutton

The "strippy" quilt was an early design that had little representation in the quilt revival of the early 1900s. One exception was the Magic Vine pattern that originated in the 1930s in a newspaper column written by Florence LaGanke Harris.

The Magic Vine is an example of how women's magazines and newspapers kept the quilting tradition alive during the Great Depression. Called the Nancy Page Club, the patterns for the Magic Vine were printed weekly along with a fictitious story about a quilt group that had Nancy Page as its leader. Each column would detail the discussions by the women about what colors to use for each floral design and other quilt related topics.

Our circa 1930 inspiration quilt is from the collection of one of our members. It has four vertical vines with 22 different floral designs bordered by a curving vine and leaves. The appliqué is all hand done.

The study quilt is based on The Magic Vine Quilt pattern designed by Eleanor Burns and published in 2007. It uses a quick turn appliqué method with non-woven interfacing. The appliqué pieces were then hand sewn in place. Reproduction fabrics from the

1930s were used throughout the quilt. Embroidery and buttons were added for embellishment, giving the study quilt a thoroughly modern look.

At one of the Repiecers' quilt study group meetings, one of the group members shared the original newspaper columns that showed the floral patterns, as well as additional information on other Nancy Page designs. Our quilt study group meets every other month at the Quilt in A Day shop in San Marcos, which is owned by Eleanor Burns.

Drezden Daizies

30" x 40"

Greta VanDenBerg
Oak Shade, Pennsylvania

Early 20th century Dresden Plate quilts are made of wedges sewn together to form a complete circle, which is appliquéd to a fabric block. In researching the history of the pattern, I discovered many early American quilts that may have inspired this Colonial Revival design.

The earliest example, found in The Wadsworth Antheneum Museum of Art collection, is a medallion quilt. It is inscribed, "Anna Tuels Her Bedquilt Given to her by her Mother in the Year AU 23. 1785." In the center of the quilt is one wedge-pieced circle applied to a background square with hearts in the corners. The circle pattern was not repeated in this quilt.

Throughout the 19th century, there are numerous examples of quilts with wedge-pieced wheels, though many appear to be four fans sewn together to form the circle. One early example found was in The Quilt Index. "Worsted Quilt, Dresden Plate" made by Martha Elizabeth Brooks Randolph, c. 1876-1900, is made of wool pieces that are foundation pieced into four sections sewn together to create a circle. The circle pattern is repeated nine times.

Inspiration for my study quilt comes from an unfinished quilt top in my collection that appears to have been started during the Great Depression. However, unlike most Dresden Plate quilts with wheels appliquéd to square blocks, the wheels are all appliquéd onto one large background piece. In 40+ years as a quilter inspired by antique quilts, this quilt top was only the second Dresden Plate quilt I have seen assembled in this manner.

It is that unusual trait that I opted to mimic with my study quilt. However, it took a long time to find just the right fabric for the center. As luck would have it, a Pratt's feed sack found me in an antique mall. In the spirit of early 20th century quilters, who "made do or did without," I cut the printed panel from the front of the bag and used the remaining fabric for the outer border. I separated it from the center with a narrow border of the same reproduction print I used to replace a damaged border on the original top.

As an "inspired by" quilt, I further connected my study quilt to the original by way of camera, computer and printer. I photographed each of the 13 original wheels so that I could print them on fabric. (Yes, 13! It appears that the unfinished quilt was intended to have 16 plates.) I machine appliquéd each piece of my design onto the quilt sandwich thus completing much of the quilting at the same time. I then filled the open background space with additional machine quilted designs similar to how I plan to finish the original top – someday!

Babies of Mine

29" x 39"

Wendy Caton Reed
Bath, Maine

I made my first quilt at the age of nine under the gentle guidance of my neighbor, Arzetta Poole (1888-1979). I have such fond memories of her simple appliqués in beautiful 1930s colors. I found my little inspiration quilt in a "junk" store in 1992 in the same town where I grew up (Edgecomb, Maine). There was no provenance with the piece but I secretly wished that I had saved a little bit of Mrs. Poole when I rescued it from a heap on the floor of a dusty back room.

I began the reproduction process by photocopying each block and then hand drawing patterns of each individual animal. I used all of the original designs except the beaver. I couldn't make it look like it belonged on a baby quilt, so I added another kitten. I mimicked the black buttonhole stitch around each appliqué, but simplified the other embroidery. I used scraps from my extensive vintage feed sack collection for the animals and vintage white feed sacks for the background. The original quilt is tied with a cotton blanket for batting and there is a wide "blanket" type binding which is machine applied. I chose to hand quilt the reproduction and used a "split" wool batting. The backing is a reproduction cotton fabric and I finished with a small separately applied binding.

I have wanted to participate in the AQSG quilt study for a long time. This seemed to be the perfect time to "jump in" and I appreciate the opportunity to help carry on this tradition.

When I first heard about the AQSG Colonial Revival Quilt Study, I began looking for a quilt to interpret. Looking through many choices in the libraries of museums, I found a four-block quilt of a Whig Rose at the International Quilt Study Center. It was a perfect choice, as I have a passion for red and green quilts.

I started my project by drawing my design on muslin to create the proper scale and then transferred the design by placing the pieces on my fabric with a light box. After struggling with the center points, I machine pieced the outer center circle and hand appliquéd the center circle.

Most interesting was the history I learned about the Whig Rose pattern. Before women could vote they supported their political party through the arts. One of these arts was quilting.

It has truly been a learning experience to work on this interpretation.

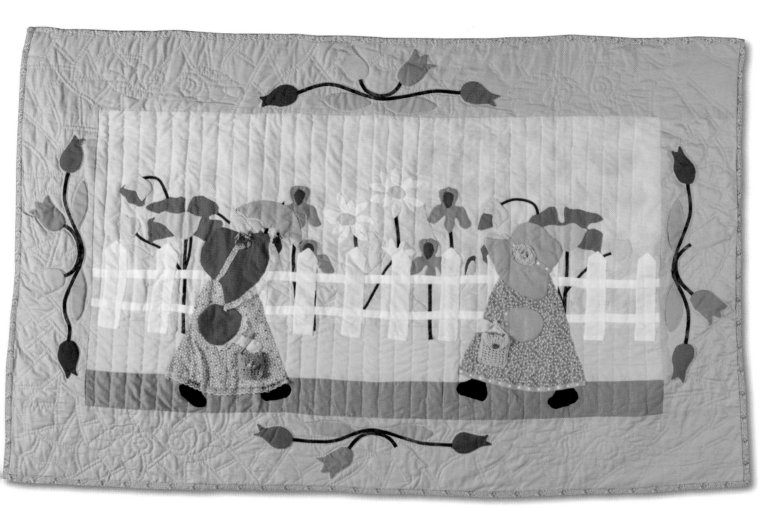

HOMAGE TO MARIE WEBSTER

34" x 55"

June McCauley Ross
Georgetown, South Carolina

I joined the American Quilt Study Group back in the day because
of my interest in quilt history. Circumstances have not allowed me to
attend any of the seminars but I have tried to remain connected by
participating in the various quilt study projects.

I chose to honor Marie Webster, who in my mind is "Miss Colonial
Revival." Her patterns opened up the quilt world to millions.

I tried to incorporate many of her patterns into one scenario. It is
important to me as a designer to not directly copy someone else's idea
but to be a faithful interpreter.

Revival!
PATTERNS

   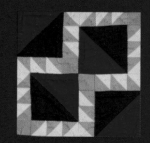

Block A (Airplane)

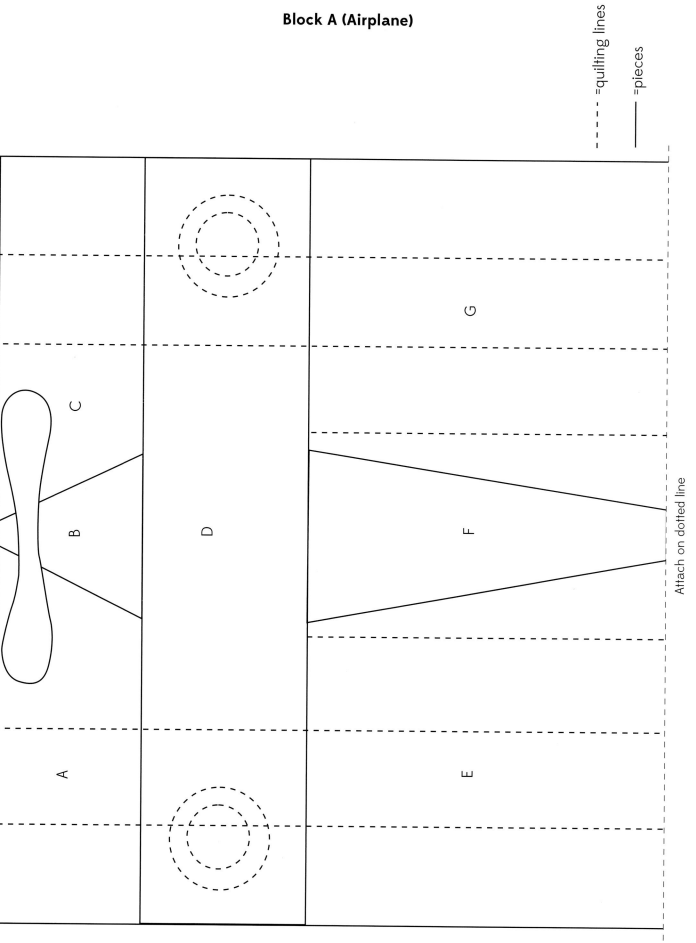

- - - - = quilting lines

———— = pieces

Attach on dotted line

(continued on next page)

BLOCK ASSEMBLY

Block A
Assemble the pieces using the Block Diagram (pages 49-50) as a guide:

- Sew A to B, then B to C, press seams to the darker color.

- This should measure 8 ½" x 2". Sew this to D and press.

- Sew E to F, then F to G and press seams to the airplane color. This piece should measure 8 ½" x 4 ¼".

- Sew this to D and press the seams.

- Sew H to I, then I to J.

- Sew K to L, then K to I and J. *Note, this is an inset seam.*

- Press all the seams to the airplane color. This piece should measure 8 ½" x 1 ½".

- Sew this to the E-F-G piece and press.

- Appliqué propeller to the block.

- Repeat with all 6 blocks.

Block B (Eagle)
Template is on pages 51 and 52.

- Use 6 - 10" x 10" squares of Fabric 1.

- Trace the eagle in the center of each block.

- Note that these will be trimmed to 8 ½" x 8 ½" after the embroidery is complete.

- Use an outline / stem stitch to embroider the eagles.

INNER QUILT ASSEMBLY

- Sew the blocks together as shown in the Assembly Diagram (page 53).

- This quilt center should measure 24 ½" x 32 ½".

Inner Border
- Using the Fabric 1 - 2 ½" strips, measure and add borders (see General Directions, page 45).

Outer Border
- Use the Fabric 2 – 2 ½" strips, measure and add borders as above.

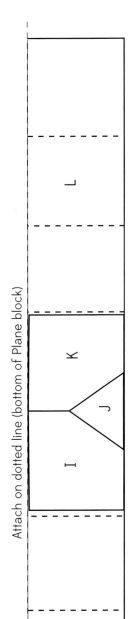

Attach on dotted line (bottom of Plane block)

Block B (Eagle)

Attach on dotted line

(continued on next page)

QUILTING

Make the quilt sandwich (backing, batting, quilt top) and baste or pin. The eagle blocks are quilted along the outer edge of the eagle embroidery and along the lower edge of the internal feathers.

The airplane blocks are quilted in the background (white) with vertical lines 1" apart, 3 on each side below the wing, and 2 on each side 1" and 2" in from the edge above the wing. Additionally, outline quilt the nose of the airplane. On each side of the wing, in pink, quilt a roundel (circle) the size of a quarter. If desired, a second smaller circle can be quilted inside the first.

The border is quilted in a 1" grid, white thread in the white border and pink thread in the pink border. The lines parallel to the borders start ½" in from the edge, such that there are 2 parallel lines in each of the 2" borders.

Quilted in white thread

Quilted in pink thread

FINISHING

Prairie Points

- Once the quilting is complete, trim the edges of the quilt.

- There are a number of methods used to attach prairie points. Because I wanted the quilting to go to the edge of the quilt, I used the method below. The edge of the quilt is a bit thicker because the batting is doubled where it is folded over. I preferred this over having the quilting stop an inch from the edge of the top to accommodate the other method of attaching prairie points.

- Fold the squares cut for prairie points in half diagonally and press. Fold them in half again and press.

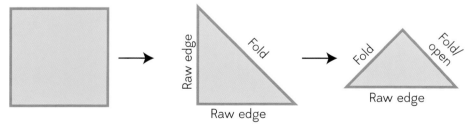

Arrange, then pin the raw edge of the prairie points along the edge of the quilt starting at one corner:

- 20 (I only used 17) across the top and the bottom.

- 26 (I only used 22) along each side. Slide them inside each other on the open side, overlapping by half.

- Once they are arranged evenly, stitch them down.

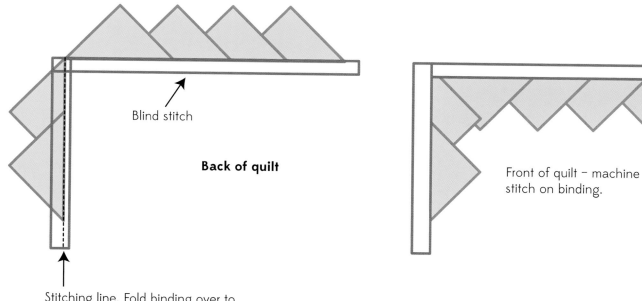

Blind stitch

Back of quilt

Front of quilt – machine stitch on binding.

Stitching line. Fold binding over to back and blind stitch down

Binding

- Cut 4 strips 2" of fabric for the binding.

- This binding will not be seen on the quilt front. Fold the 4 strips in half, press.

- Attach this in the same manner you would a regular binding, however, sew each strip separately to each side, just to the corner, leaving about ¼" to tuck under.

- Fold the binding back away from the prairie points.

- Fold the prairie points back so they frame the quilt and blind stitch the binding to the back of the quilt.

- Blind stitch.

ASSEMBLY DIAGRAM

SUMMER ROSE

Marjorie Farquharson
Needham, Massachusetts

"English Rose Variation" made by Olive McClure Cook, appeals to me in so many ways. The appliqué, the design, the color, the fabrics, and the originality of her work intrigue me. Her four-block English Rose quilt truly harkens back to quilters of the 19th century whose quilts were often inspiration for early Colonial Revival quilts.

When I created my version, I decided to stay true to Olive's quilt and bring my own esthetic to my work. My first decision was to include all of the design in my study quilt by keeping it a four-block design with borders. One change that I made was to eliminate the scalloped edge. I chose to work within the same color palette that Olive used. Once I began choosing my fabrics, the quilt became my own. Since using toile has become a characteristic of my quiltmaking, I chose a subdued toile for my background fabric. Another important fabric decision was to use a green fabric with shading and a design for the vines and leaves. As I studied Olive's colors in her flowers and buds, I enjoyed looking at her combinations and placement. While I used her yellows, oranges and reds, I added more shades and a greater number of fabrics than the study quilt. When I added some small touches of bright orange, purple and another green, my quilt glowed.

As I made my quilt, I often thought about Olive. She must have loved to appliqué, as do I. She was an older woman, making her quilt in 1939 in the midst of the Depression. She must have certainly made thoughtful fabric choices and played with the placement of her colors, just as I did. I wondered why she made one border design different from the other three. The top border is more delicate with many circles for buds or berries. The other borders are more substantial, and their design echoes that of the middle vines. Did she make that one different border first and decide that it was too delicate or difficult? Or, did she make it last to add a difference in the design? Either way, it adds personality to her quilt.

It's almost as if Olive gave me a cutting from her own garden that I was able to nurture and foster. Thus, the name for my quilt is "Summer Rose."

SUMMER ROSE

These instructions are for a quilt that measures 48" x 48".

FABRIC REQUIREMENTS

3 yards light for background
1 yard green for leaves and vines
Assorted fabric for appliqué: 8–10 medium and dark fabrics – ¼ yard each
½ yard red for binding

CUTTING DIRECTIONS

From Background Fabric:
4 – 26" x 26" for blocks

From Green Fabric:
4 Large flowers, bottom layer
16 Swags
16 Corner flowers, bottom layer and stem
2 Center vine bud stems
22 Center vine flowers, bottom layer and stem
15 Side and bottom border flowers, bottom layer and stem
14 Side and bottom border bud stems
7 Top border bud stems
¼" bias for vine: total of 9 ½ yards

From Assorted Fabrics:
4 Large flowers (6 pieces, vary fabrics for contrast)
16 Corner flowers (6 pieces, vary fabrics for contrast)
22 Center vine flowers (3–4 pieces, vary fabrics
   for contrast)
2 Center vine buds
15 Side and bottom border flowers (2 pieces)
14 Side and bottom border buds
26 Top border berries
7 Top border buds

From Red Fabric:
6 – 2 ½" strips for binding

BLOCK ASSEMBLY

Trim blocks to 24 ½" x 24 ½". Sew the 4 background blocks together in a four-patch.

APPLIQUÉ

Arrange the center appliqué vines, buds and flowers across the seam lines. Arrange the appliqué for the 4 blocks. Stitch in place using your favorite appliqué method.

Last, arrange the border appliqué. Start with the bottom border appliqué, then the side, then the top. Stitch all in place using your favorite appliqué method.

> **TIP:** Appliqué the layers together from the center down before stitching the entire layered piece to the background block.

FINISHING

Quilt as desired and bind.

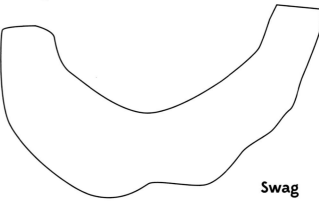

Swag

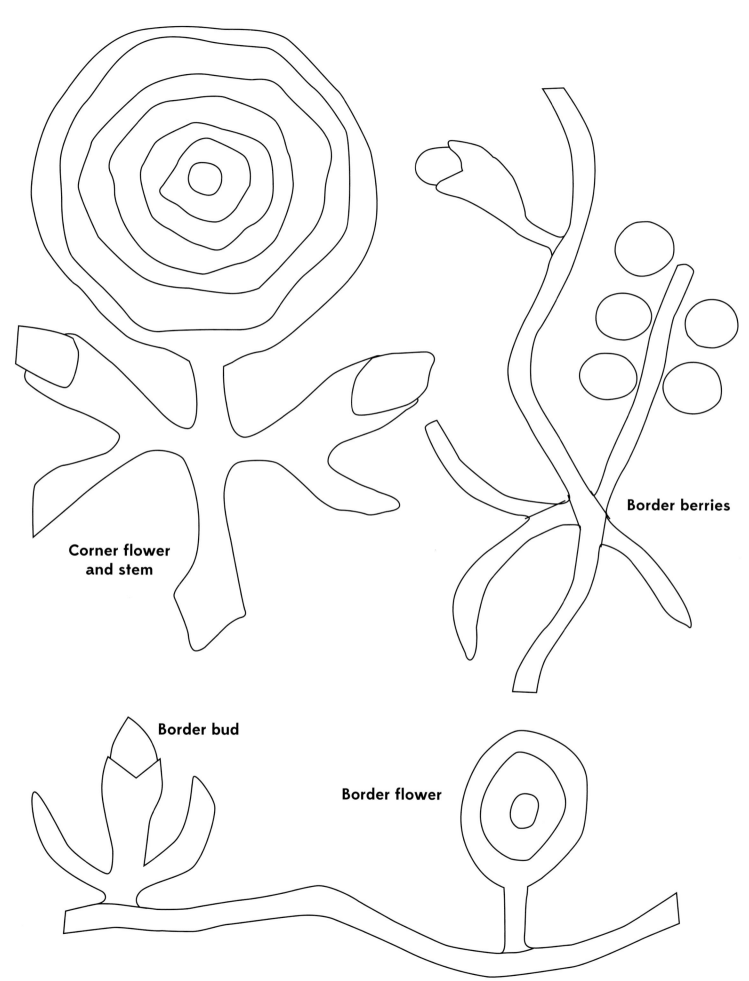

**Corner flower
and stem**

Border berries

Border bud

Border flower

57

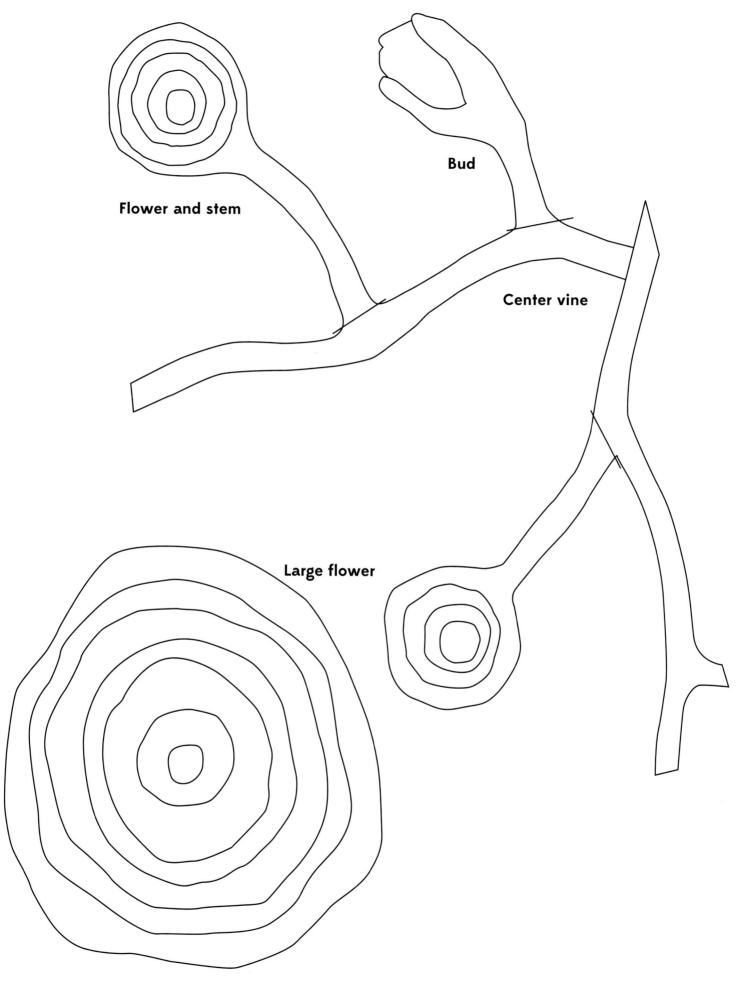

Flower and stem

Bud

Center vine

Large flower

FLOWER BASKET

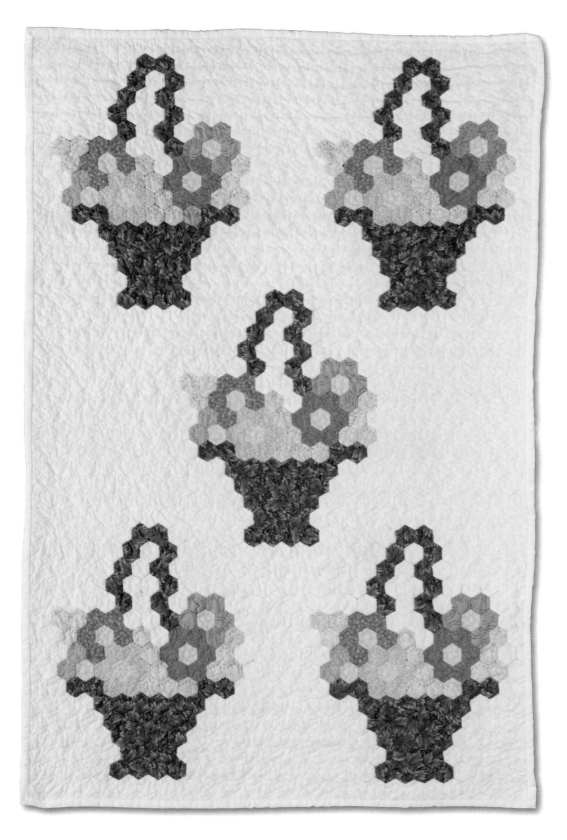

Catherine Noll Litwinow
Bettendorf, Iowa

I like the wonderful soft pastel fabrics from the Colonial Revival Era. The quilt I originally chose was an Ann Orr-like design with one inch squares forming the design. On a closer look, I discovered that a one inch grid had been quilted on the whole top. Then every single one inch square was appliquéd to make the design! It was an easy choice to pick a hexagon quilt with one inch hexagons.

The original quilt had 32 baskets. I decided to make a smaller piece. I wanted something that I could piece when I traveled. One difference between the quilts was my desire to use prints rather than solids. I wanted to use colors that matched the original quilt. Finding just the right colors was a challenge, even with wonderful reproduction fabrics. I purchased many more yards of fabrics than I needed.

I have a great appreciation for the quilters who use quarter inch hexagons! My fingers would ache if I basted for several hours. It would have been so boring making the hundreds of white hexagons. I varied the white on white hexagons for more variety.

The monotony of basting the fabric over papers, then whip stitching the hexagon together is an activity that leads to meditation. For me, doing the five baskets was enough.

I often procrastinate. It was true with this project. So when January 2012 rolled around it became clear that Ann Orr quilting design would never be completed, even in miniature. I decided to quilt my piece like the original. Only the top of the hexagons were quilted—horizontal quilting goes very fast.

How to Make This Quilt

Flower Basket

These instructions are for a quilt that measures 23" x 34 ½".

Fabric Requirements

Dark Green: ½ yard for basket
Light Green: ¼ yard for leaves
Yellow: ⅛ yard for flower centers
Orange: ⅛ yard
Dark Blue: ⅛ yard
Pink: ⅛ yard
Purple: ⅛ yard
Light Blue: ⅛ yard
White: 3 yards for background and binding

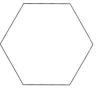

Template

Cutting Directions

Note: a 1 ½" square makes one hexagon.
Dark Green: 185 – 1 ½" squares
Light Green: 65 – 1 ½" squares
Yellow: 25 – 1 ½" squares
Orange: 10 – 1 ½" squares
Dark Blue: 25 – 1 ½" squares
Pink: 30 – 1 ½" squares
Purple: 30 – 1 ½" squares
Light Blue: 25 – 1 ½" squares
White: 847 – 1 ½" squares
         3 – 2 ½" x WOF strips for binding

Block Assembly

Using either the template provided or purchased English paper pieces (½" hexagons), hand piece the hexagon pieces together as shown in the Block Diagram.

Quilt Assembly

Continue piecing background hexagons in the amounts shown in the Assembly Diagram to join blocks into top.

Trim edges to create a straight line for binding.

> **Note:** One of the baskets in Catherine's quilt contains two pink flowers (instead of one pink and one light blue). Can you find it? Catherine reports, "Yes, the two pink flowers are deliberate. Double pink is my favorite quilting color and fabric and most of the AQSG study quilts I've made contain double pink. So, I used two pink flowers to equal double pink." (groan - quilter humor)

Resource
Paper Pieces
P.O. Box 68, Sycamore, IL 60178
(800) 337-2900
www.paperpieces.com

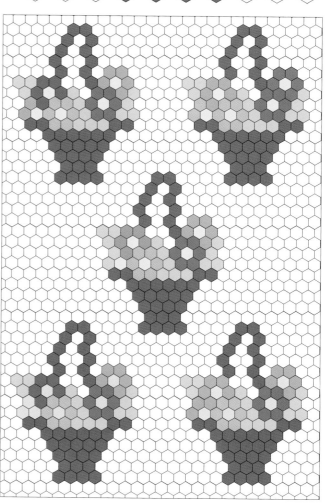

Assembly Diagram

Irish Bear Paw Puzzle

Florence McConnell
Manteca, California

I love quilts with striking color and strong visual impact and found my inspiration quilt, "Solid Geometric Quilt: circa 1920, Pennsylvania" on Stella Rubin's website. I was intrigued by the optical illusion created by the small blocks set side by side using this color palette. The blocks appear misaligned but they are not. The triangle border with the separate lavender binding adds a clever and interesting finish to the quilt.

I became interested in identifying the name of the block and searching for other quilts using a triangle, separately bound border. I found two versions of the block in the 1928 edition of *Ladies Art Company*; one named Irish Puzzle and the other named Bear's Paw. Next, an internet search of Irish Puzzle produced an article by Beth Donaldson giving the history of the Irish Puzzle block. Beth indicated she found both versions in the 1895 edition of *Ladies Art Company*. In addition, Beth stated Ruth Finley gave Irish Puzzle 13 other names in 1929 and The Kansas City Star published it five times in 1931 under five of the names published by Finley.

A search for quilts made with a triangle-shaped, separately bound border revealed a number of quilts finished with a prairie point border but I was unable to find one with a separate bound triangle border. Clearly the maker of my inspiration quilt was a creative woman.

From my research I concluded my inspiration quilt reflects the 20th century Colonial Revival trend of "taking the old and making the new" with new names and updated color schemes. My reproduction was machine pieced and hand quilted.

How to Make This Quilt

IRISH BEAR PAW PUZZLE

These instructions are for a quilt that measures 36 ¾" x 52 ¾".

FABRIC REQUIREMENTS

Fabric 1: 1 ⅜ yard light for bear "claws"
Fabric 2: 1 ⅜ yard medium for bear "claws"
Fabric 3: 1 ¾ yards medium dark for bear "paw" and triangle border
Fabric 4: 1 ¾ yards dark for bear "paw" and triangle border
Fabric 5: ⅓ yard light for small square
Fabric 6: ⅓ yard

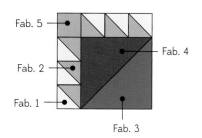

Cutting Directions

From Fabric 1:
288 – 2" x 2" squares for HST method 1 *or*
3 – 18" x 22" rectangles for HST method 2
From Fabric 2:
288 – 2" x 2" squares for HST method 1 *or*
3 – 18" x 22" rectangles for HST method 2
From Fabric 3:
48 – 4" x 4" squares for HST method 1 *or*
2 – 16" x 24" rectangles for HST method 2
From Fabric 4:
48 – 4" x 4" squares for HST method 1 *or*
2 – 16" x 24" rectangles for HST method 2
From Fabric 5:
4 – 1 ½" strips, cut into 96 - 1 ½" squares

Refer to General Directions on page 45 for HST methods.

Block Assembly

Unit A

- Use the 288 - 2" x 2" squares of Fabric 1 and Fabric 2 for HST method 1 or use the 18" x 22" rectangles of Fabric 1 and Fabric 2 with a 9 x 11 grid of 2" for HST method 2 to make 576 half-square triangle units.

- Trim each to 1 ½" x 1 ½".

Unit B

- Use the 48 - 4" x 4" squares of Fabric 3 and Fabric 4 for HST method 1 or use the 16" x 24" rectangles of Fabric 3 and Fabric 4 with a 4 x 6 grid of 4" for HST method 2 to make 96 half-square triangle units.

- Trim each to 3 ½" x 3 ½".

Unit C

- Sew 3 Unit A pieces together.

- Sew another 3 Unit A pieces together, each turned one-quarter turn.

- Add one Fabric 5 square as shown.

- Attach to Unit B as shown, watching placement of the half-square triangle strips.

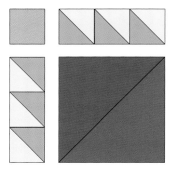

- Unit C should measure 4 ½" x 4 ½".

- Make 96 Unit C sections.

Complete Block

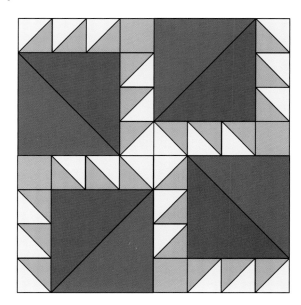

- Sew 4 Unit C sections together, turning each one-quarter turn. Repeat to make 24 blocks.

Border

Cutting Directions

From Fabric 3:
Cut 40 triangles using template A.
From Fabric 4:
Cut 40 triangles using template A.
From Fabric 6:
Cut 40 – 1 ¼" x 7" binding strips.

Assembly

Binding Strips

- Press strips wrong sides together.

Unit D

- With wrong sides together, place 2 Fabric 3 triangles together with a binding strip lined up with fabric edges on 1 side of triangle.

- Sew binding to 1 side of triangle. Press.

- Sew binding to second side of triangle. Press.

- Stitch binding down on back of triangle, similar to adding quilt binding.

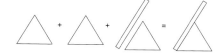

- Repeat with remaining Fabric 3 triangles to make 20 triangles.

Unit E

- With wrong sides together, place 2 Fabric 4 triangles together with a binding strip lined up with fabric edges on 1 side of triangle.

- Sew binding to 1 side of triangle. Press.

- Sew binding to second side of triangle. Press.

- Stitch binding down on back of triangle, similar to adding quilt binding.

- Repeat with remaining Fabric 4 triangles to make 20 triangles.

Template A

Adding the Border

- Arrange triangles around quilt top with open edges even with quilt top edge.

- Alternating Unit D and Unit E triangles, overlapping slightly at base.

- Stitch with ¼" seam.

- Press the back of the border.

Finishing

- Quilt as desired.

- To finish after quilting, turn quilt top edge and back under ¼" and blind stitch along seam line of triangles to create a knife edge finish.

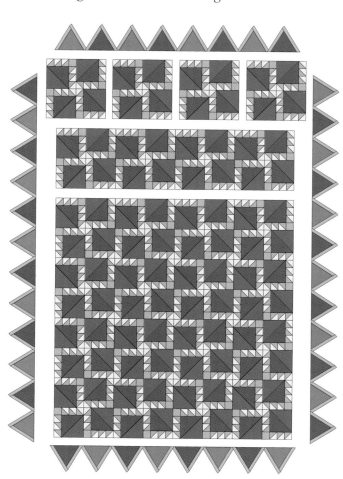

ASSEMBLY DIAGRAM

MORNING GLORY BASKET

Judith Thompson
Wenonah, New Jersey

PASSIONATE ABOUT POPPIES

Sandy Sutton
Seal Beach, California

Marie Webster was an extraordinary woman. She was a quilt designer, businesswoman, and author of the first American book about quilting, *Quilts, Their Story and How to Make Them*, originally published in 1915 and reprinted many times, the latest being 2009.

It could be argued that Marie Webster singlehandedly set the Colonial Revival quilt period in motion with dozens of beautiful floral designs executed in pastel colors. These reflected the Arts & Crafts Movement of the early 1900s but were often medallion designs with wonderful borders, harkening back to some of the earliest quilt motifs in America.

Her designs appeared in the *Ladies Home Journal*, and she was asked to write articles about quilts. After many requests for her quilt patterns she published a catalog entitled "The New Patch-work Patterns." She founded her own business, The Practical Patchwork Company, in 1921. Besides patterns, the company also sold partially completed quilts.

To honor the impact of this extraordinary entrepreneur, I selected her Poppy Quilt design from a quilt in my collection that was made in Ohio. On the reverse of the quilt is stated: "Jessie Ringrose Carson to my daughter Margaret Carson Hunt 1930." As a native Californian, I am partial to this design as the poppy is our state flower. The original quilt is beautifully executed with tiny appliqué stitches and quilting at 13 – 14 stitches per inch.

The pattern for this quilt is in Marie Webster's *Garden of Quilts*, by Rosalind Webster Perry and Marty Frolli. I reduced the pattern by 50% to fit the study quilt size criteria. This pattern first appeared in the January 1912 *Ladies Home Journal*.

As I worked on the study quilt, I learned that Jessie Carson had made some changes to the poppies to make them easier to appliqué. So it seemed appropriate for me to make additional changes in the study quilt, redesigning one of the leaves to facilitate the appliqué work, and embroidering the stems to replicate the tiny poppy stems on the original quilt. I also tried to mirror the beautiful quilting on the original quilt, but Jessie's stitches were far smaller than mine.

The beautiful appliqué designs from Marie Webster are timeless in their appeal. I thank her for her visionary work in carrying our quilt history forward.

POPPY

These instructions are for a quilt that measures 41 ½" x 47".

FABRIC REQUIREMENTS

Fabric 1: 2 ⅓ yards light for background
Fabric 2: ⅝ yard medium for poppy petals (yellow in quilt pictured)
Fabric 3: 1 yard dark for poppy petals (orange in quilt pictured)
Fabric 4: 1 ½ yards medium/dark for leaves, border and binding
Embroidery floss to match Fabric 4

CUTTING DIRECTIONS

From Fabric 1:
4 – 11" x 13 ¾" for Block A
22 – 7" x 10 ½" for Block B
4 – 7" x 7" for Block C
3 – ¾" x WOF for 2nd inner border

From Fabric 2:
4 – ¾" x WOF for 1st and 3rd inner border
4 – Template A
4 – Template A reversed
22 – Template B
8 – Template E

From Fabric 3:
4 – Template C
4 – Template C reversed
22 – Template D
12 – Template F
30 – Template G

From Fabric 4:
5 – 2" x WOF for outer border
12 – Template J
30 – Template K
30 – Template L
8 – Template M
8 – Template M reversed
22 – Template N
22 – Template N reversed
5 – 2 ½" x WOF for binding

BLOCK ASSEMBLY

- Using your favorite appliqué method, complete the appliqué blocks as shown on block diagrams.

- Note that 2 of Block A are done from the lower right corner and two from the lower left corner (in reverse).

Block A:

Reversed

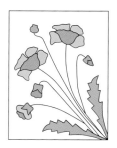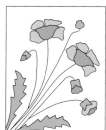

Reversed

- Embroider stems.

- Trim block A to 10" x 12 ¾".

- Trim block B to 6" x 9 ½".

- Trim block C to 6" x 6".

QUILT ASSEMBLY

- Sew the blocks together as shown to create the center medallion, turning each block to create design.

- Using ¾" strips of Fabrics 1 and 2, measure and add borders as shown on page 45.

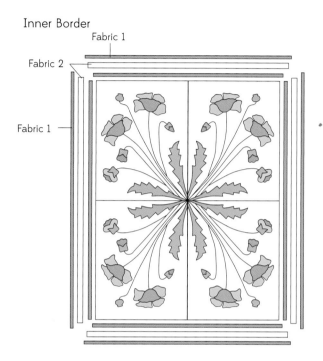

Inner Border

Fabric 1

Fabric 2

Fabric 1

- Sew together 5 Block B for each short side and 6 for each long side.

- Sew Block B units to medallion unit and miter the corners.

- Set in corner Block C.

- Using 2" strips of Fabric 4, measure and add the border as shown on page 45.

FINISHING

Quilt as desired and bind.

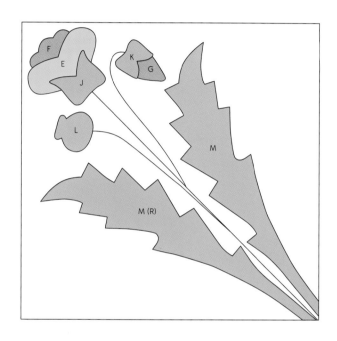

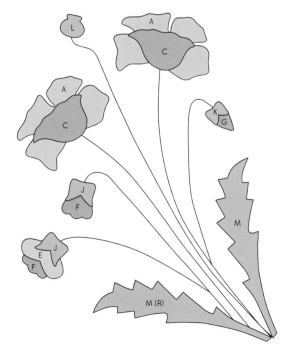

Make 2 blocks like this and 2 blocks using A (R) and C (R).

A

D

E

F

G

J

B

K

L

C

M

N

B (R)

D

L

K

G

N (R)

N

76

GUILT TRIP

Xenia Cord
Kokomo, Indiana

Although I have participated in every quilt study proposed by AQSG, this time I felt I had enough on my plate without making a special quilt for the Colonial Revival study. Then, at the end of April 2012, a quilt study committee member asked why I wasn't participating, and guilt set in.

I have always liked "Trip Around the World" quilts but had never attempted one, preferring to buy rather than build. But with the

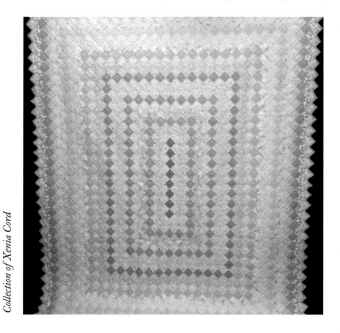

short time remaining to me, a small version seemed possible. So I was inspired by expedience and guilt. My Featherweight and I struggled through the construction, building and attaching sets of four color coordinated fabrics, one after another. The original had 2" squares; in order to conform to the study's size limits, I opted for 1" pieces (finished). I quickly realized that I could never make this pattern in my usual king size!

The original quiltmaker quilted inside each of the squares in her quilt, avoiding the problems presented by the hundreds of seams and intersections. My squares were too small for that approach, so I decided to divide them on the diagonal. Shortly after I began that process I realized that the result would be a ½" grid over the entire surface and a confrontation with every intersection. There's a saying, "Well begun is half done." Don't you believe it!

Whoever she was, my original quiltmaker struggled with the inside/outside corners presented by the natural edges on her quilt, and her binding is less than satisfactory.

At least that was a problem I could anticipate, so as I quilted, I mentally devised a way to achieve a more effective finished edge. In my own mind the process seemed flawless; possibly my result mirrors hers!

PS - The fabric in the outer row of squares, the binding, and the sleeve was designed by AQSG member Julia Zgliniec, whose imprint is on the exposed selvage of the sleeve.

Guilt Trip

These instructions are for a quilt that measures 38" x 48".

Fabric Requirements

There are **7 color families needed** for this quilt. Traditionally, the quilt would have contained the following for each color family. Note that the 7th color family, consisting of only three fabrics is used for the center:

A – a light print
B – a medium print
C – a solid
D – a print containing the color from the solid and from the next color family.

Fabric 1A: ¼ yard	**Fabric 2A:** ¼ yard	**Fabric 3A:** ¼ yard	**Fabric 4A:** ⅛ yard
Fabric 1B: ¼ yard	**Fabric 2B:** ¼ yard	**Fabric 3B:** ¼ yard	**Fabric 4B:** ⅛ yard
Fabric 1C: ¼ yard	**Fabric 2C:** ¼ yard	**Fabric 3C:** ¼ yard	**Fabric 4C:** ⅛ yard
Fabric 1D: ¼ yard	**Fabric 2D:** ¼ yard	**Fabric 3D:** ⅛ yard	**Fabric 4D:** ⅛ yard

Fabric 5A: ⅛ yard	**Fabric 6A:** ⅛ yard	**Fabric 7A:** ⅛ yard	**Binding:** ⅓ yard
Fabric 5B: ⅛ yard	**Fabric 6B:** ⅛ yard	**Fabric 7B:** ⅛ yard	
Fabric 5C: ⅛ yard	**Fabric 6C:** ⅛ yard	**Fabric 7C:** ⅛ yard	
Fabric 5D: ⅛ yard	**Fabric 6D:** ⅛ yard		

Cutting Directions

- For each fabric cut 1 ½" x WOF strips

- For binding, cut 4 – 2 ½" x WOF strips

Sewing Directions

Step 1

- Sew together 4 sets of strips 1A / 1B / 1C / 1D.

- Cut 1 ½" across the strips.

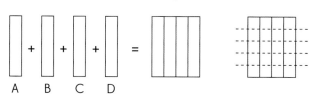

- From the remaining Fabric 1A-C strips, cut 1 ½" squares and sew together as shown.

- Repeat with Fabric 2A-D, Fabric 3A-D, Fabric 4A-D, Fabric 5A-D, and Fabric 6A-D.

- From Fabric 7A: Cut 22 – 1 ½" squares, Fabric 7B: Cut 18 – 1 ½" squares and Fabric 7C: Cut 8 – 1 ½" squares. The diagrams will show which squares to stitch to the end of the rows.

Step 2

- Sew together the sections made in Step 1 to make rows as shown in the diagrams on pages 80 and 81.

- Press the seams in opposite directions for each row.

1A	1B	1C	1D	+	2A	2B	2C	2D

Quilt Assembly

Unit 1
Make 4 of these units. (There will be an additional row added to 2 of the units to create Unit 2.)

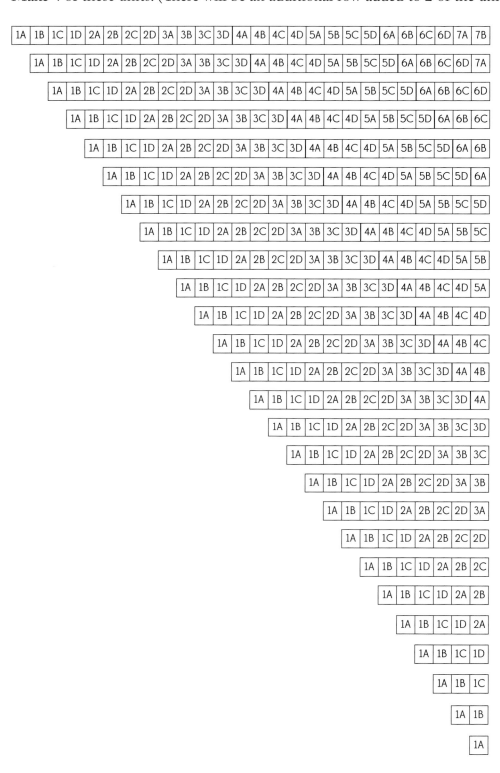

Unit 2
Stitch together two of the following rows. Add the row to the top of 2 of the Unit 1s.

| Fab 1 | Fab 2 | Fab 3 | Fab 4 | Fab 5 | Fab 6 | +7A/7B/7C |

Unit 3

Make 2 of these units.

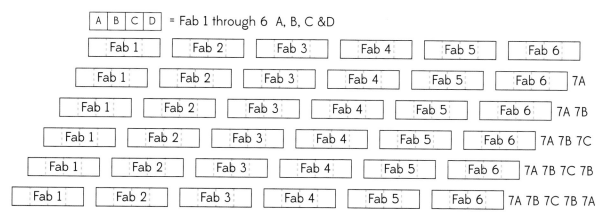

Refer to the Assembly Diagram and stitch the units together.

FINISHING

Quilt as desired and bind. Xenia painstakingly stitched her backing to her quilt top and stitched, trimmed and turned it to match the edges of the outer row of blocks. Her quilt is hand quilted in a grid pattern.

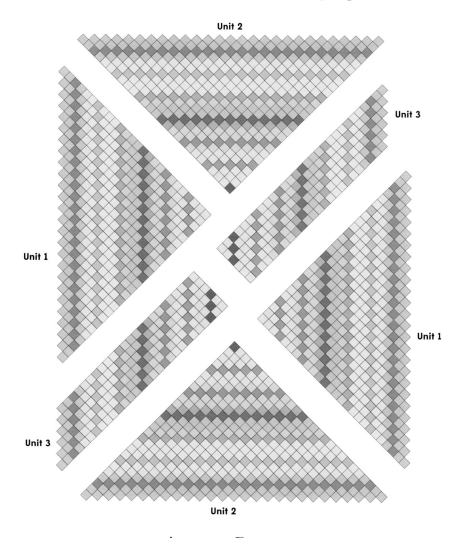

ASSEMBLY DIAGRAM

DOUBLE NINE PATCH

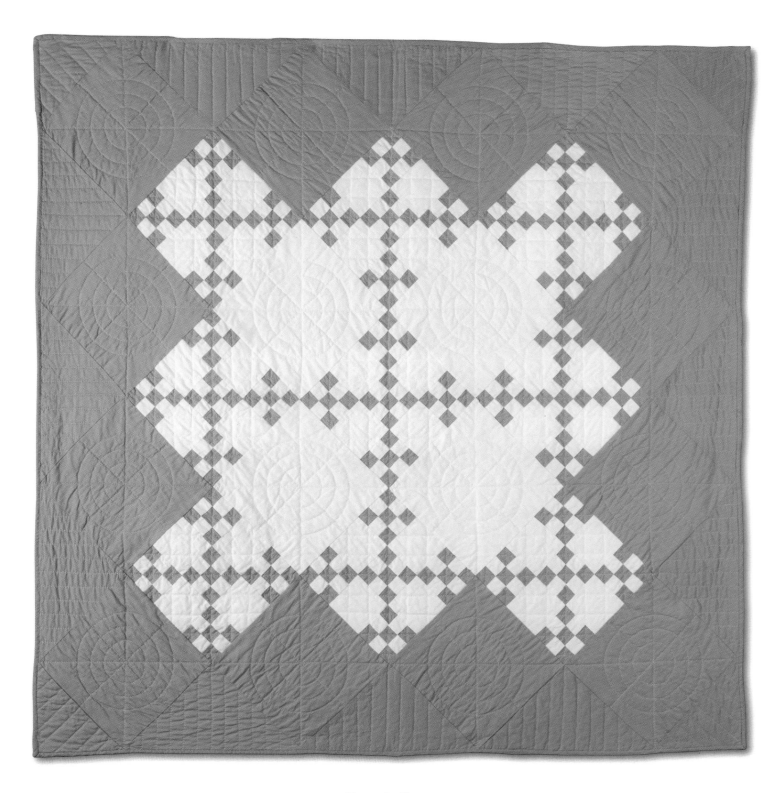

Pamela Pampe
Winchester, Virginia

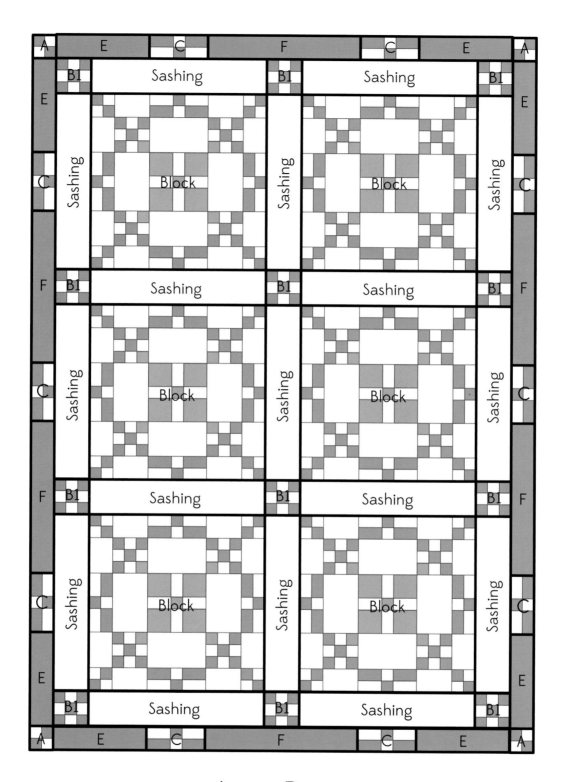

ASSEMBLY DIAGRAM

Summer Arbor

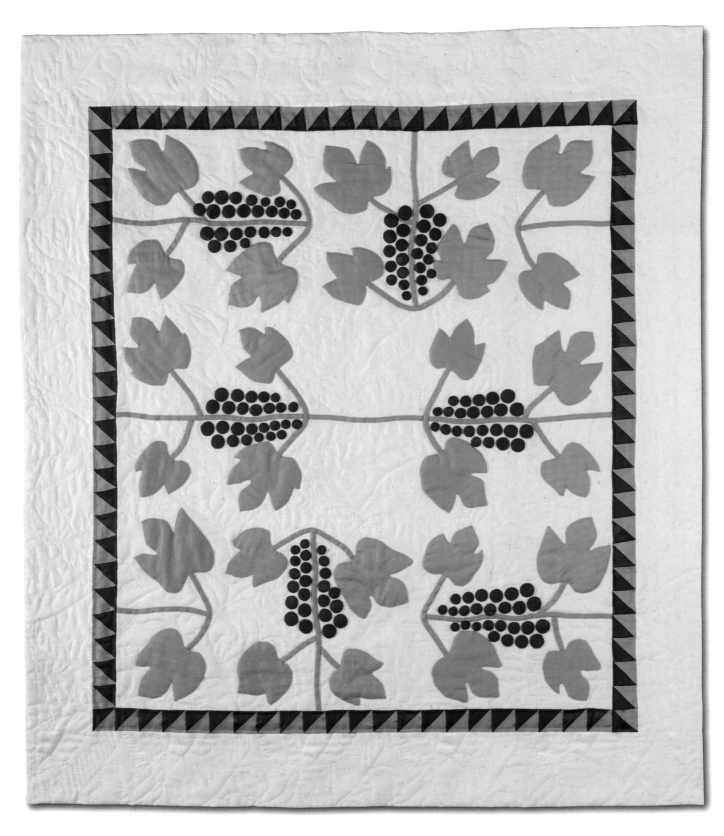

Nancy Ostman
Groton, New York

My study quilt appeared like a sunlit summer arbor on my computer screen. While I realized my view was not true to the original, I decided to go with that glowing mental image. Leafy silks from a recycled fabric shop added shimmer for the background and grapes, and an African brocade provided a bit of pixilation for the leaves.

I appreciated the variation in leaf shapes on the original quilt, and thus cut and sewed my leaves and vines freely. Making the quilt mostly in Canada at our summer cottage, I stepped back a century in terms of technology. Pressing grapes on a table leaf over two chairs with a stove-heated oven, I wondered if prohibition was in effect when the original quilter worked. I eyed our Old Home treadle machine and wondered if it was up to the task. I thought about rural electrification and wondered whether the quiltmaker was eager for easier ways to do things, or content to work carefully on a few projects.

How to Make This Quilt

SUMMER ARBOR

These instructions are for a quilt that measures 43" x 49".

FABRIC REQUIREMENTS

Fabric 1: 2 ½ yards light for background
Fabric 2: ½ yard dark for grapes and inner border
Fabric 3: 1 ⅜ yard medium for leaves and inner border

CUTTING DIRECTIONS
Refer to General Directions on page 45 for HST methods.

From Fabric 1:
6 – 14" x 14" for Block A
3 – 8" x 14" for Block B and Block C
5 - 5 ½" x WOF for outer border
6 – 2 ½" x WOF for binding

From Fabric 2:
46 – 2 ½" x 2 ½" for HST method 1 *or* 1 - 16" x 21" rectangle for HST method 2
144 grapes

From Fabric 3:
46 – 2 ½" x 2 ½" for HST method 1 *or* 1 - 16" x 21" rectangle for HST method 2
14 – Leaf A
14 – Leaf B
½ yard - to make approximately 180" of ¼" bias strips for vine

BLOCK ASSEMBLY

- Using your favorite appliqué method, complete appliqué blocks as shown on block diagram.

- Add appliqué vine across Block C matching up to the other blocks.

- Note: variety in the leaves is intended and will help them look more natural. You can reverse the leaves or slightly change the shape to achieve this look.

- Trim block A to 12 ½" x 12 ½".

- Trim block B and C to 6 ½" x 12 ½".

CENTER QUILT ASSEMBLY

Sew the blocks together as shown in the diagram, turning blocks to match the pictured quilt.

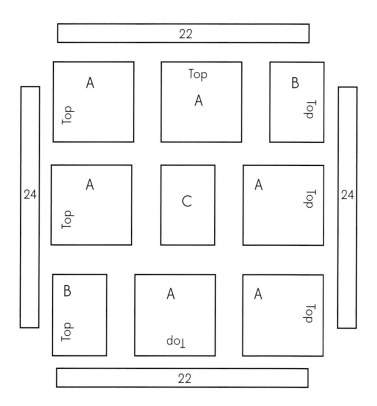

BLOCK ASSEMBLY DIAGRAM

BORDER ASSEMBLY

Inner Border

- Use the 46 – 2 ½" x 2 ½" squares of Fabric 1 and Fabric 2 for HST method 1 or use the 16" x 21" rectangles of Fabric 1 and Fabric 2 with a 6 x 8 grid of 2 ½" for HST method 2 to make 92 half-square triangle units.

- Trim each to 2" x 2".

- Sew 22 together to add to the top and bottom.

- Sew 24 together to add to the sides.

ASSEMBLY DIAGRAM

Outer Border

Using 5 ½" strips, measure and add borders as shown on page 45.

Quilt as desired and bind.

Attach on dotted line

B

Block A

Block A Top

A

Attach on dotted line

Block A Top

Join

Attach on dotted line

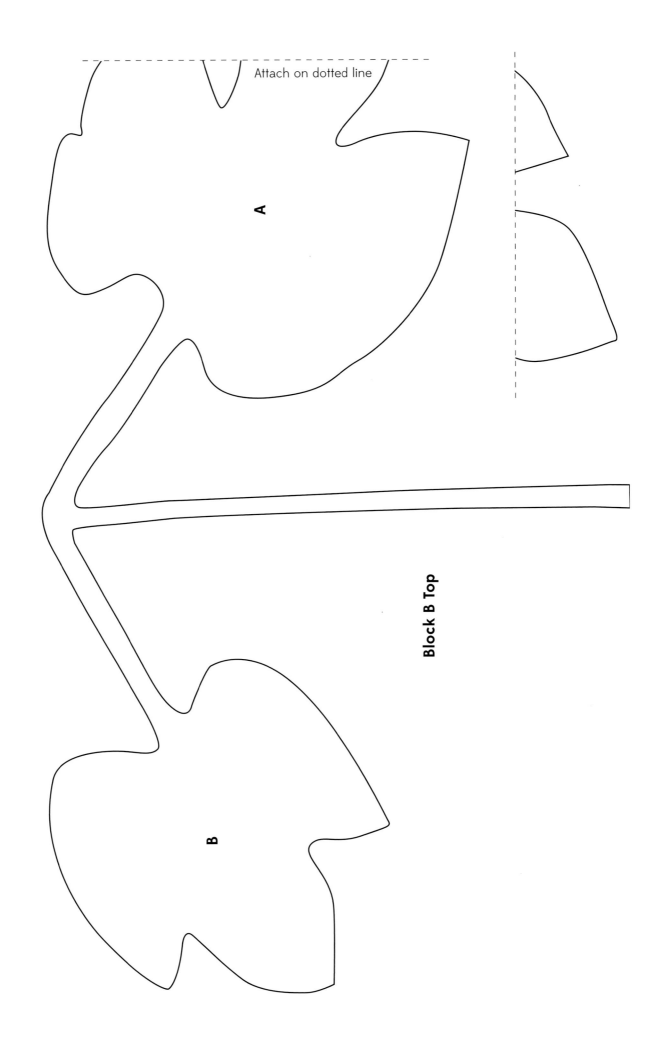

Attach on dotted line

A

B

Block B Top

94

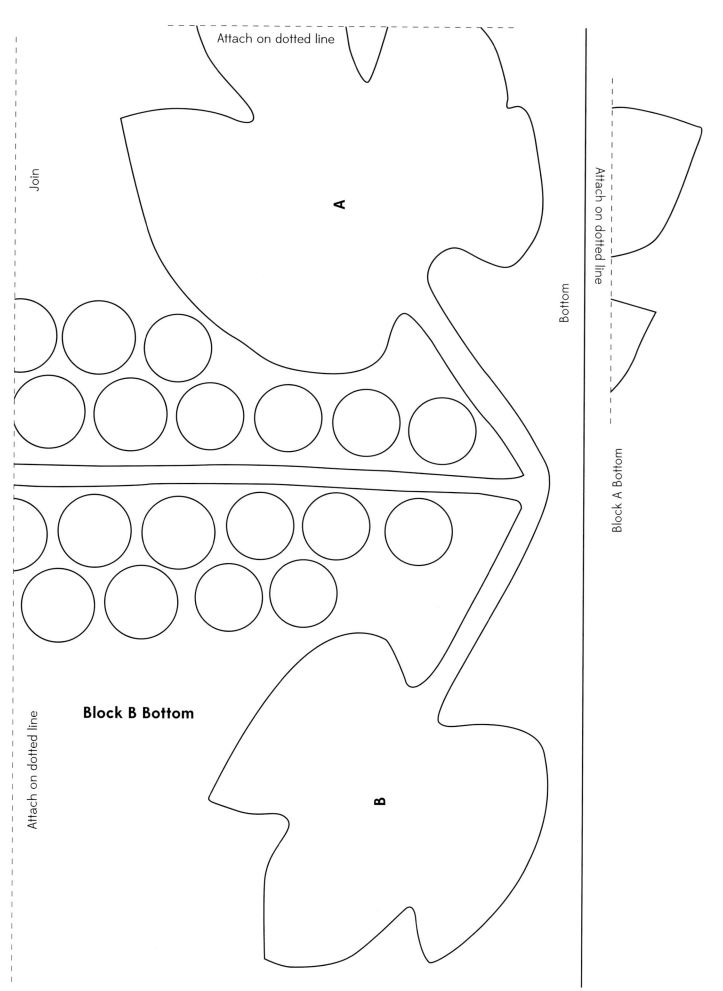

Attach on dotted line

Join

A

Attach on dotted line

Bottom

Block A Bottom

Block B Bottom

Attach on dotted line

B

Attach on dotted line

95

The American Quilt Study Group is believed to be the oldest and largest member organization dedicated to quilt-related studies in the world.

The American Quilt Study Group is a non-profit quilt research organization with more than 1,000 members in the U.S. and abroad. Founded in 1980 in Mill Valley, California, by Sally Garoutte with a small group gathered around Sally's kitchen table, AQSG has grown into a unique and highly respected international organization.

The American Quilt Study Group sets standards for quilt studies, and provides opportunities to increase knowledge about quilts and textiles, their history and their place in society. American Quilt Study Group members encompass all age groups and include quilters and non-quilters alike. Membership is comprised of traditional and contemporary quilt artists, quilt lovers, historians, researchers, collectors, dealers, folklorists, authors, museum curators, quilt appraisers, and students of women's studies.

If you are interested in quilts and quilting, their history and role in society, and you would like to help promote and preserve this traditional yet ever-changing art, join us!

Members of AQSG participate in the effort to preserve quilt heritage through our various publications, extensive research opportunities, yearly Seminar and membership contacts.

Your membership includes *Blanket Statements*, a quarterly newsletter; *Uncoverings*, an annual journal of the papers presented at our Seminar; research information; the opportunity to join our Yahoo Groups chat list and the opportunity to attend our yearly Seminar.

Levels of Membership Support include:

$75 Friend
$65 Senior (65+)
$55 Student (full-time)
$120 Associate
$120 Corporation/Organization

Canada please add $5.50 for postage; all other countries please add $19 for postage.

American Quilt Study Group
1610 L Street
Lincoln, NE 68508

WWW.AMERICANQUILTSTUDYGROUP.ORG

 Become a fan of American Quilt Study Group on Facebook.